Be Your Dog's Best Friend

John Rogerson

Popular Dogs
London

Popular Dogs Publishing Co. Ltd

An imprint of the Random Century Group
20 Vauxhall Bridge Road
London SW1V 2SA

Random Century Australia (Pty) Ltd
20 Alfred Street, Milsons Point, Sydney 2061

Random Century New Zealand Ltd
191 Archers Road, PO Box 40-086, Auckland 10

Random Century South Africa (Pty) Ltd
PO Box 337, Bergvlei 2012, South Africa

First published 1992

A catalogue record for this book is available upon request from the British Library

ISBN 0 09 177123 4

My grateful thanks to Dolores Palmer and Joyce Thurman,
both dedicated teachers, who helped to translate my
'adult' manuscript into a format suitable for
younger readers.

John Rogerson 1992

Printed in Great Britain
by Scotprint Ltd, Musselburgh

Contents

1 Dogs through the ages

The pet dogs that live with us today are quite unlike their wild ancestors, which were wolves. Long ago when people first took young, wild dogs into their homes, the partnership became a two-way affair; people and dogs were able to give a great deal to their common friendship. People were able to offer their pet dog food, warmth and shelter, whilst the dogs were able in return to offer their skills at running and hunting. The dogs had such a wonderful sense of smell and they were able to hear things that their owner could not. So the dogs became as valuable to their owners as a spear or a bow and arrow. That our dogs' distant relations were used for hunting we know from cave paintings, which clearly show dogs that are helping their owners to hunt for food.

As people became better at growing their own crops and rearing wild goats, sheep and pigs, the work of some dogs began to change. Dogs that had previously been selected for their hunting ability were not in quite as much demand.

So a new type of dog was wanted. This meant that any dogs which had shown a flair for herding animals were carefully chosen. It was hoped that these dogs would produce puppies which could be used to look after flocks of sheep and herds of goats that roamed from one area to another in order to get the best grazing.

In addition to the herding skill, people wanted dogs that would protect the valuable domestic animals from hungry wolves. This is how guard dogs were originally developed: not to guard people but to guard their flocks.

Dogs have different abilities, just as people do. Dogs that possessed certain useful skills tended to be put together to produce puppies. These puppies were likely to possess the skills of their parents. This is known as selective breeding. Most of the breeds of dogs that we have today were first bred to carry out a particular job of work for the people with whom they lived. Even though your dog may not possess these skills to the same degree as his ancestors, they are still there. These skills make him the sort of dog that he is.

Breeds of dogs are usually described by placing them into groups so that it becomes easy to see what types of dog were used for which purpose.

The Working Group

You herd— I'll guard

In this group we find dogs like the German Shepherd (Alsatian), the Border Collie and the Old English Sheepdog. These dogs were bred mainly for herding and guarding and could travel long distances, sometimes over rough land. This meant that although they were perhaps not as fast as some of the other breeds, they had terrific powers of endurance.

The Gundog Group

Here we find breeds such as the Golden Retriever, Pointer, Irish Setter and Cocker Spaniel. These breeds were developed from the early hunting dogs. They were selected for their ability to find game and indicate this to their owners. Then they had to bring it back after it had been hit by spear, bow and arrow or gun. Not all gundogs were first bred with hunting in mind. The Labrador Retriever, for instance, was first developed for plunging into icy cold waters to fetch fish that had slipped from fishermen's nets into the sea.

The Hound Group

Dogs in this group were used for hunting in the open country and they usually hunted in packs. Dogs in this group, such as Greyhounds and Salukis, generally run very fast over a short distance. These dogs had to see a long way across the countryside when they were hunting. They vary in size from the very large Irish Wolfhound to the much smaller Beagle. There is a difference between the work of the dogs in this group and the dogs in the gundog group. In the gundog group the dogs fetched birds and animals their owner had killed. In the hound group the owners wanted the dogs to chase and kill the animals which the owners then collected.

The Terrier Group

The terrier's earliest purpose was to follow small game or animals that were classed as pests into their underground burrows. This group contains breeds such as the smooth and the wire-haired Fox Terriers, the larger Airedale and the smaller Border Terrier. These dogs are usually very agile, alert, and have lots and lots of energy. They were so bold and persistent that some of the breeds were developed for fighting one another; but thankfully this is no longer allowed by law.

The Utility Group

Er.... Um.....

This group contains all of the breeds that would be difficult to place in any other group, because they were bred for other uses and they do not fit in with any of the other groups. This group contains breeds such as the Dalmatian, the Japanese Akita and the Shar Pei (pronounced Shar Pay).

The Toy Group

DOWN BOY!

In this group we find breeds like the Cavalier King Charles Spaniel, the Papillon (sometimes known as the Butterfly Dog because of the shape of its ears) and the Yorkshire Terrier. These are all small dogs and are in this group because they were bred as pets without any purpose in mind other than to be company for their owners. As you will see from the names of these dogs, some had ancestors who were working dogs.

So you see that whichever dog you choose, even though it may have a long or a short coat, it may be large or small, it may be black, white or brown, you can be sure that it has come from one of the dogs that first lived with people, thousands of years ago. All dogs are related to one another.

2 So you want a puppy?

Of all the pet animals we have today none is as good as a dog. The dog family has always lived in small social groups or packs in the same way that people once did. So it is easy to see why people and dogs should be able to live together as a family. As we have seen, our modern breeds of pet dogs have come about because people bred dogs with certain useful skills. So when you choose a puppy you should be aware that it will be likely to have some of the skills that were thought to be important in the past. This means that you will have to choose carefully to make sure that the breed you decide to have is really the breed that you want, and can manage to raise and train successfully.

Sadly, lots of dogs that are bought as pets end up unloved and unwanted just because the owner does not realise that some breeds of dogs are not suitable for certain kinds of families. Just because a particular breed may look attractive to you does not mean that it will fit into your particular family. So how do you choose a breed that will prove suitable? Let's start by looking at the home that you live in and the type of family that you are.

How large is your house? If you live in a house where there is lots of space, then perhaps one of the larger breeds may be suitable; but remember that if you have elderly people and/or a young baby living with you then a large dog might prove to be a problem. It could accidentally bump into an old person or baby and knock them over. Larger dogs do not move as quickly as some of the smaller breeds and therefore are not quite as good at getting out of the way of Grandma or baby.

Do you have a garden, and if so how large is it? Some breeds will be happy to play in a small garden, whilst others require a much larger area in which to run around. You should also remember that even the best kept lawn can soon start to look really shabby when forty-five pounds (20 kg) of adult dog is racing around chasing a butterfly. If you do have a garden it is important that it is securely fenced to prevent your dog escaping and getting into trouble. If you do not have a garden, then this does not mean that you cannot keep a pet dog. However, you will need to take your dog out to a place where it can run about freely every day. Only a few breeds are really happy without a garden.

How much free time do you have to devote to a dog? Long-coated dogs look very beautiful in the show ring, but the amount of time necessary to keep a long, silky coat in good condition and free of tangles can sometimes add up to many hours each week. There will also be other responsibilities, such as exercise, feeding and training. If you do not have much free time, then a short-coated breed may be the best choice.

You should also think about the cost of keeping a dog for the next ten to fifteen years. First there is the price that you will have to pay for a puppy. This can be from as little as £20 for a crossbreed or mongrel from an animal welfare group up to as much as several hundred pounds for a pedigree (pure-bred) dog. Next you have the cost of feeding and vaccinations to think about. As a general rule, the larger the dog the more expensive it is to keep.

Let's now have a look at some of the different types of dog that are available so that you are able to compare one against another.

Mongrels

Crossbreeds

These are dogs that are a mixture of different breeds and it is usually impossible to tell which these are. Dogs like this can make very good pets, but it is difficult to know what size a mongrel puppy will be when it is fully grown. Also it is impossible to know what its working skills will be, unless you know both the mother and the father quite well.

These are dogs with parents of recognisable breeds but not the same breed. As with our mongrel puppy, it is difficult to tell which of its skills will come from the mother and which will come from the father. So it will be difficult to know how large it will grow or whether it will be like its mother or its father in the way it behaves.

Pedigree (pure-bred)

Buying a pedigree puppy should at least mean that you will have an idea how large it will grow, how much exercise it will need and how much it will cost to feed. However, pedigree dogs tend to have more health problems than mongrels.

Male or female?

A male dog can be a little more independent and harder to handle than a female (bitch). So a large male dog could be hard to control. Neutering is an operation done by the vet which stops the male from being able to breed. This will normally make the dog more attached to its owner and less likely

to want to play with and chase other dogs and bitches. This is the reason why guide dogs are neutered before they are one year old.

Although bitches are said to be more loving than dogs, with a bitch you will have the problem of seasons, during which she will be capable of being mated by a male dog. A season happens about every six months. During the three weeks of each season, the bitch gives off a scent which can be noticed by other male dogs in the area up to six miles away. If she is mated, a litter of puppies can be expected 63 days later. Spaying is an operation that can be carried out by a vet which will stop a bitch from coming into season and producing unwanted puppies.

Choosing a breed

When the whole family has made a decision to get a dog you will need to decide what breed (if you decide to get a pedigree) will best fit into your lives. To help you to decide you should visit your local library and borrow some books on the breeds that you like. This should help you to understand what to expect of the various breeds. You should also go along and talk to your local vet and ask for his advice on your choice of breed. It is also a good idea to visit your nearest dog training club and talk to the instructor, who should be able to tell you how easy it will be for you to handle and train your dog. Be guided by the advice that you are given, because these people will have more experience in the good and bad points of any of the breeds that you may like to own. Your puppy will be with you for many years to come. So do not be in a rush to choose a dog - just in case you spend the next fifteen years regretting the choice that you have made.

3 Choosing your puppy

When you have chosen the breed you want, you will now have to find a litter of puppies. There are several ways of doing this. You can buy a copy of one of the weekly or monthly dog magazines and look in the 'puppies for sale' columns, or you can obtain a list of breeders by contacting the Kennel Club. You could also go along to a dog show and talk to the people who are showing your chosen breed: they should be able to give you advice on where to buy a puppy. There are many different places that you can obtain a puppy from.

1.　BREED KENNELS　These kennels are usually run by people who show their dogs and so they have a reputation to protect when selling puppies. They will also have adult dogs of their own to show you which will give you some idea of how your puppy will grow up.

2.　PUPPY FARMS　You can usually spot these quite easily because they advertise for sale puppies of many different breeds. Puppy farms are not usually licensed, which means they are not looked at or inspected, and the conditions in which the puppies are kept are terrible. No one with a genuine interest in dogs will ever advise you to get a puppy from one of these places, so steer clear of them.

3.　PET SHOPS　Puppies are still sold in a few pet shops because people will see them and will buy one on impulse. You will never see the mother of the puppies, so you should never buy one from a pet shop.

4.　CASUAL BREEDERS　A breeder is defined as being the owner of a bitch at the time that she has a litter of puppies. A casual breeder is usually someone who has a pet bitch that she has had mated in order to produce a litter of puppies. The puppies will usually be raised in the house rather than in a kennel and should understand a little about family life. You can sometimes get a very good pup in this way. The question to ask the breeder is, 'Why did you have a litter of puppies from this bitch?' If they answer, 'Because we thought it would settle her down,' then be wary about buying a puppy. It may well grow up to have the same sort of problems that the breeder was trying to correct in the mother by breeding a litter from her.

5.　ANIMAL WELFARE ORGANISATIONS Usually the best place to buy a crossbreed or mongrel puppy. However, you will not often be able to see the mother and will probably never see the father so you will not be able to tell how big the puppies will grow or how they are likely to behave in adult life. The puppies themselves are usually very well cared for by such organisations. You should be able to find your nearest one by contacting your local vet.

Viewing a litter

The ten golden rules to follow are these:

1. Never buy a puppy the first time that you look at a litter. You should always make at least two visits and if possible see more than one litter before coming to a decision.

2. Always go along with all the family so that you all get the chance to see the puppies and to choose one.

3. You must see the bitch away from her puppies at first, in order to get some idea if she is friendly towards people. If she is aggressive, then it is better not to buy one of her puppies. It is likely that it will have already learnt her less than friendly behaviour towards people. This means that as the puppy grows into an adult dog it may start to become unfriendly to your friends and relations, just as its

mother was. Asking the breeder to let you watch Mum being brushed will give you some idea of how easy she is to handle. If the breeder cannot brush the bitch, then her puppies may prove difficult to handle when they grow up.

4. If the bitch is friendly when she is by herself, then you can go in with all the family to where the puppies are. The bitch should be happy about you touching any of her puppies. It is better not to pick any of them up because it is very easy to drop one accidentally. If the bitch becomes unfriendly when you go near the puppies then you should not buy one but find another litter.

5. Always encourage the puppies to come towards you by tapping your fingers on the floor gently. Never chase the puppies around or try to grab at them.

6. If any of the puppies will not come anywhere near you, do not feel sorry for them. Simply ignore them and choose a puppy from one of the bolder ones.

7. If any of the bolder puppies tries to push in for attention when you are stroking any of the other pups, do not choose that puppy. This applies particularly if they start to bite or growl at the puppies that are getting in the way. They are known as dominant pups and may prove to be too headstrong for you, or any of your family, to handle easily.

8. Ask the breeder to remove any of the puppies that are too shy or too pushy. If you are looking for a bitch puppy, ask the breeder to remove all the dog puppies. If you are looking for a dog puppy, ask for the bitch puppies to be removed.

9. Now that you have reduced your choice down to two or three puppies you can pick the one that you all like the look of. However, what will most likely happen is that one of these pups will choose you as its new owner.

10. Never be tempted to take two puppies home as company for one another. This is almost certain to lead to problems as the two puppies grow - problems that will prove extremely difficult to correct at a later stage. It is also advisable not to buy a puppy over the age of sixteen weeks. If it has been kept with a litter brother or sister or its mother it will not have had much contact with people and could be difficult to live with.

When you finally decide on the puppy that you want, the breeder should give you all the following information:

1. Pedigree form which gives details of your puppy's 'family tree'.
2. Registration transfer form (if it is a pedigree dog) so that you can transfer the puppy into your name with the Kennel Club. ONLY the breeder can register the pup with the Kennel Club.

COME ON YOU TWO —WALKIES!...

So if you are not given this form, you will not be able to have your pup registered in your name.

3. Details about vaccination against the most important dog diseases.

4. Information on the type of diet that the puppy is being fed. A diet sheet giving amounts and feed times. You should obtain a supply of the same food prior to collecting your puppy.

5. Details about worming which will keep your puppy healthy. Your puppy should already have been wormed once before you buy it.

6. Ask about insurance for your puppy. Most breeders have a short-term insurance on the puppies which will go towards paying the vet's bills should the puppy become ill. Your parents can continue to pay the insurance, which means that they will not have to worry about paying the bills if your puppy is ill or has an accident.

Finally ask the breeder to brush your puppy so that you can satisfy yourself that it is used to being brushed and has already learned to accept this. If the breeder cannot manage to brush this pup then it is unlikely that you will be successful either. This will make it difficult for your vet to examine the puppy or your friends to stroke it.

If all goes well and you finally decide that you want to take one of the puppies home, then do not do so right away but wait for a day or two. This will give you time to prepare the things that you need to make your new puppy welcome in your home.

Just before you leave for home hand the breeder a piece of soft blanket, around half a metre square, and ask for this to be placed in the puppies' sleeping area. It will absorb the smell of that area. Remember to collect it when you go to fetch your puppy in two days' time.

4 The early weeks

By the time the big day arrives you should already have all the necessary things to ensure that your new puppy settles in happily and comfortably in its new home. The list of equipment should include such things as separate food and water bowls, and a soft puppy collar and lead. You will also need a bed or basket for it to lie in. The breeder will tell you the right kind of brush and comb to buy. You should have a supply of the food that the puppy is used to eating and a small selection of toys for it.

When you collect your puppy be sure to collect the piece of bedding material that has been lying in the puppies' sleeping area for the past two days. You will need this later, and so you should place it in a polythene bag and tie a knot at the top to seal it from the air.

If the journey home is by car, you should put a large cardboard box on the back seat and place your puppy in that. By all means put your hand in the box and stroke the puppy whilst you are being driven home but it is important that you do not take the puppy out to sit on your lap. If this happens then it may well think that this is where it is allowed to sit on all future journeys. This will make car travel difficult when it is fully grown.

When you get your puppy home it is a good idea to take it outside in the garden and allow it to run around in case it wants to relieve itself before going into your house.

In the next few weeks you, and the rest of the family, must teach your puppy the rules of the family in which it now finds itself. Look upon your puppy's life in the same way that you would look upon a new book. There may be a few words already written on the first page which tell us about the puppy's family and what it has learnt from its mother, brothers and sisters. The rest of the book is full of blank pages on which you must write out the rest of its life. What your puppy learns is what you are going to teach it. If you do not take the time and trouble to teach your puppy, then it will not know how to behave.

Your puppy has no idea of what is right and what is wrong. You must teach it these values. Your puppy cannot think in quite the same way that you and I do. The puppy learns by playing. Its mother will have taught the puppy some things already. Your puppy depends on you in the same way that you depended on your parents, when you were a baby.

House-training

Most puppies are very easy to house-train if a few simple rules are kept to:

1. There are three danger times when a puppy will want to go to the toilet:

(a) Immediately after it has been fed.

(b) As soon as it wakes up, even if it has only been asleep for a few minutes.

(c) Whenever it can be seen running around in circles sniffing at the floor.

As soon as you see any of these happen, take your puppy out to where you want it to go to the toilet. Make a fuss of it as soon as it does. Then it will soon learn to go on that spot and will be less likely to relieve itself in the house.

2. When you go to bed at night you must put some layers of newspapers on top of a sheet of polythene so that the floor under the newspapers does not get wet if your puppy wants to go to the toilet. Puppies are not able to last right through the night until they are several months old. It is unkind to tell them off for doing anything on the floor when left overnight, because it is not really their fault.

3. The newspapers should only be put down at night and when the pup will be left alone in the house for a short period of time. They should be placed near the door and away from the puppy's sleeping area.

4. If your puppy misses the papers then you should clean up any soiled areas using a special liquid which you can get from your vet. This liquid will remove the smell so that the puppy is less likely to foul that area again.

5. Never smack your puppy or, worse still, rub its nose in what it has done. That will only make it frightened of you, and that is the last thing that you want. Remember that if your puppy relieves itself in the house it is your fault for not watching it more closely.

Sleeping

It is not a good idea to allow your puppy to sleep in your bedroom, no matter how much you want it to. It will be far better with its own sleeping area, provided it is dry and warm. It is the first few nights that are usually the worst, because the puppy will be all alone and will miss the company of its brothers and sisters. You can help it to settle in more quickly by playing with it for a while before it goes to bed so that it is tired. You should then take your puppy outside to where it is allowed to go to the toilet and after that bring it back into the house. Place in the puppy's bed the piece of material that the breeder has kept in the puppies' sleeping area. Turn out the light and quietly close the door, leaving it in the room that it is to sleep in. Because the room is dark your puppy should use its terrific sense of smell to find the bed that smells of its previous family. Then it should soon settle down to sleep. If it makes a noise it is better to ignore this. If you go back to it, the next time you leave the puppy it will bark and howl even louder.

It is also important to insist that the puppy gets used to being left in the room where its bed is for a few minutes at a time every single day. It will then know that it cannot follow you around all the time. Puppies that are never left by themselves when the owners are in the house grow up into adult dogs that refuse to be left by themselves. They either bark and annoy neighbours or chew up the furniture. Start as you mean to go on. If your puppy does not accept being by itself after a few nights you could try a cassette tape that has been designed to calm and relax your puppy. Your vet will advise you on this.

When you do go in to see your puppy in the morning, try to ignore it for the first few seconds. Otherwise it will get over-excited and expect that everyone who comes into the room will make a fuss and play with it. If you allow this to happen then you will soon find that your puppy will get excited and jump up at anyone that walks in. Your puppy will then become difficult to control.

Grooming

One of the most important things to do with your puppy each day is to brush it. This should be done before it is fed and before you play with it. Your puppy must be brushed in the way that you were shown by the breeder. This is just as important for short-coated breeds as it is for the long-coated ones. Brushing gets the puppy used to being handled and touched when you want to do so. Lots of adult dogs become difficult

to control simply because they were not taught to keep still and be brushed when they were puppies and could be handled easily.

Games

All games between you and your puppy must only take place when there is a grown-up with you. The puppy must not start to play games that will get it into trouble when it gets older. All toys are best kept under your control, so that you can decide when to play and what games to play. Your puppy can be allowed to have things like a large rawhide chew or a sterilised marrowbone on which to exercise its teeth and gums. Games are covered in more detail in the next chapter.

Socialising

So that your puppy grows up to be friendly towards other people and dogs in your area it is important that it is socialised correctly. Socialising means taking your puppy out to meet people and other animals so that your pup is not worried about them when it gets older. The best way of doing this is to ask your vet about the puppy playgroup nearest to where you live. These playgroups are run in order to teach puppies to be friendly with adults, children and other puppies. The whole family will be welcome to attend. The earlier you can enrol with your puppy the better it will be for it. It is important that you do not leave this until the puppy is over sixteen weeks of age.

Rules

During the first few weeks with the puppy it is important that you write down all the rules that you want your puppy to learn. Then everyone in the house will be using the same set. It is unfair on the puppy if one person teaches it that it is all right to jump up but the next person tells it off for doing just that. It would also be terrible to punish a puppy for breaking a rule that it did not know or understand.

5 Training your puppy

Your puppy should be trained because this will increase your enjoyment in owning it. The training should lead to a greater understanding between the two of you. Your parents will have the greater part of the responsibility for training your puppy, just as they have had in providing your education. However, it is important that you help to train the puppy as much as you can so that the puppy responds to you as well as to Mum and Dad.

There are two ways that we can train a dog. One way is by shouting and telling it off every time that it is disobedient. This is the way that lots of puppies are trained and you can imagine how sad this will make your puppy. Think what life would be like for you if your parents shouted at you and slapped you every day and hardly had a kind word to say to you. The second, and best, way to train your puppy is by teaching it that if it does as you tell it then it will get some special treats or rewards. There are different kinds of rewards:

1. We can stroke the puppy, which we call physical praise.
2. We can tell the puppy what a good dog it is in an excited tone of voice, which we call verbal praise.
3. We can also play with the puppy with a favourite toy.
4. We can give the puppy a food treat such as a doggy choc drop.

All training works on the idea that if your dog does something and gets a reward it will be more likely to do the same thing again, hoping to get the same reward. It works like this: if you tell your dog to sit and then say 'Good dog', at the same time giving it a biscuit, the next time your puppy hears you tell it to sit it will be more willing to do so because it should remember that something nice happened the last time that it sat when you told it.

The only problem is that your puppy will sometimes learn to do the wrong things just because it thinks that you are rewarding it. Suppose that you walk into the house after school and your puppy jumps up to greet you. You then tell it that it is not to jump up and scratch you with its nails, and you push it back down to the floor. Remember that your puppy likes you to speak to it and touch it and that is exactly the reward that it got from you for jumping up. You touched it and spoke to it. This means that the next time that you come in your puppy will jump up even more to get you to touch and speak to it. Your puppy does not understand our language. So it is up to you and your parents to teach it the meaning of a few simple words that we call commands.

The words that are most commonly used as commands are listed below, along with what they should mean to your puppy.

'COME' - meaning that you want your puppy to come to you straight away, no matter what it is doing and no matter what else is happening at the same time.

'SIT' - meaning that your puppy is to place its bottom on the floor and remain in this sitting position until you tell it that it can move.

'STAY' - meaning that your puppy must stop where it is until you return and allow it to move.

'HEEL' - meaning that your puppy is to walk on the lead alongside you without pulling.

'DOWN' - meaning that your puppy is to lie down and stay there until you tell it that it may move.

Remember that when you start training you will have to teach your puppy the meaning of all these words which will be new to it. This means that you will have to be very patient and repeat the lessons until it understands what is required.

You should now refer to your wall-chart 'TRAINING YOUR DOG' (free from Pedigree Petfoods Education Centre, address on Page 64), which explains how to teach these important basic commands.

The training should be carried out in order, teaching only one exercise at a time. Move on to the next exercise when your puppy is confidently obeying the command that you are teaching.

As young dogs are not able to concentrate for long periods, you should keep all training sessions very short to avoid boredom setting in. It is important that you train your puppy for just two minutes each time. Do this two or three times a day. You can gradually increase your training time as your puppy's concentration improves with age.

All training sessions should be carried out when a grown-up is there to help you. This means that you will have to plan your training sessions to take place with your parents present. Training can be done both at home and at a dog training club that allows junior handlers to train their dogs.

Dogs, like children, all learn at different speeds and are sometimes better at some subjects than others. You must make sure that you do not get angry or appear to be in a bad mood if your puppy has difficulty in learning any of the commands. It is usually a good idea to ask a grown-up to take over training the puppy in any of the exercises that you find difficult at any particular session. This is so that your puppy finishes the session successfully and happily.

Training should take place every day so that your puppy does not forget any of its lessons. If you miss a day, this may make it more difficult for your puppy to learn what you want him to do.

Training should be fun for both you and your dog. If it isn't, then your puppy will not look forward to its training sessions. During a training session you should check to see if its tail is wagging. If it isn't, your puppy will not be enjoying it: this means that you will have to think carefully about the type of reward that you are using, and change it for something better.

Playing games

The games that you play with your puppy will help it to learn what is the right and wrong thing to do. This is very important for times when your puppy is feeling playful. It must learn the right way to play with you. I have listed some common games and suggested some rules that you might like to teach your puppy.

Chasing games

These games should be played by throwing a toy for the pup to chase and bring back. When you first start to play this game it will be unlikely that your pup will want to bring the toy back to you, because it will think

that you are going to take it away. If this happens, do not chase the puppy, because it will think that this is part of the game and it will be more difficult for you to teach your puppy to bring things back to you. Simply sit still and wait for your puppy to lie down and play with the toy on its own. When your puppy does this, slowly walk over to it and gently stroke it. Do not try to take the toy away from your puppy. Wait until the puppy drops the toy. When you have the toy, walk away from the pup and then throw the toy again. After a few times your puppy should always head for the same spot to lie down with the toy.

When this happens it is a simple matter to go and sit in that spot and, hey presto, you should find that your puppy brings the toy straight back to you. Always remember to stroke and praise the puppy before you take the toy away to throw it again.

You must never let the pup play games of chasing you around. Otherwise the puppy may feel that it is all right to chase other children, and that will get it into trouble when it grows into an adult dog.

Tugging games

You must only play this game with your puppy after your parents have taught it the rules of the game. It is also very important that both your parents are present when you play this game. Tug-of-war is a game of strength between you and your puppy and so it is vital that it learns that you are stronger than it is. This means that you will have to win the game more times than your dog does. It may also mean that Mum and Dad will have to help you to win the first few times that you play it. Then the puppy will not think that it can bully you when it gets bigger and stronger.

The rules that you should have learned BEFORE you play this game are:
1.   No growling.
2.   You must win by getting the toy away from your puppy more times than it is allowed to win the toy from you.
3.   At the end of the game you must win the toy and put it away so that your puppy cannot get it by itself.
4.   Your puppy is only ever allowed to put its teeth on the toy during the game. Your puppy should never be allowed to tug playfully at your clothing or to nip your fingers.
5. If your puppy is already too strong for you, then your parents should hold onto the toy with you so that the puppy cannot pull you over.

Wrestling games

These are games where you roll around and wrestle on the floor. There is a danger that your puppy will think that you are another dog. Your puppy may bite your face or catch one of your eyes with its needle-sharp teeth. You should never play this sort of game.

Of course there are many other games that you can play with your puppy, using a favourite toy. As long as you are the one that sets all the rules of the game, then you and your puppy should continue to enjoy playing together. If you do not set all the rules at the beginning, then your pup may invent its own rules: this may make play sessions very difficult for you both.

6 Bad behaviour

Many adult dogs that behave badly do so simply because their owners have taught them to. Remember what we said earlier that if a certain action is rewarded, then that action tends to happen more often. In many cases of bad behaviour the dog is simply doing what it knows will bring a reward. Take food stealing, for instance.

If you leave your puppy in a room where it can reach a plate of chocolate biscuits, it may smell them and then jump up and eat them. If you then come back into the room and say 'Who's done that?' and tell your puppy off, it will be unlikely to understand that it is being told off for eating the biscuits. The puppy will think that it is being told off because you have come back into the room and said 'Who's done that?'. This means that the next time that your puppy is left alone in that room it will jump up and look for food because it was rewarded by finding something nice to eat the last time that it did that. When you walk back into the room and say 'Who's done that?' your puppy will run away or cower. This is because the last time that you did this it was shouted at. In a short space of time the puppy will start to get worried every time that you walk into the room and say 'Who's done that?' even if it has not touched any food or jumped up at the table.

Let's now look at some common behaviour problems and see why the dogs behave in the way that they do.

Chewing when left alone

There are many reasons why dogs chew furniture when they are left on their own. The most common reason is to prevent their owners from leaving them alone in the house. It begins like this: the puppy is given lots of toys to play with, some of which are things like old slippers or gloves. The owners play with the puppy with these toys for a few weeks and then cannot be bothered to play quite as much as they did at first. The puppy then tries to get the owners to play with an old slipper. When they refuse, the puppy starts to play with the slipper by itself and starts to chew it. The owners ignore this. The puppy puts that slipper down and picks up a new slipper and starts to chew it. The owners immediately start to chase the puppy around to get this slipper from it. What the puppy has just learnt is that when the owners refuse to play, if it starts to chew a new slipper then they suddenly do want to play. The puppy has learnt that chewing gets it attention at times when no one is taking any notice of it. When the puppy is then left by itself it begins to chew the furniture or carpets. Sooner or later the owner walks in and takes the puppy to what it has chewed and then tells it off. The puppy now knows that it is what it has chewed that has caused its owner to come back and give it some attention. The next time it is left alone the puppy chews even more in order to get its owner to return more quickly.

You can see now why it is important that you do not give the puppy things to chew and to play with that are similar to the things that he is not allowed to touch. If the puppy does start to chew at the carpet or furniture when you are in the room, do not chase it around and tell it off. Instead you can try throwing something soft and heavy at the puppy, like a small cushion that will give it a mild 'shock' when it hits it. Try not to let the puppy know that this has come from you and it will quickly learn that if it chews the furniture then something unpleasant happens. This is known as ENVIRONMENTAL CORRECTION, which means that the 'shock' came from what the puppy was doing and not from you. When the puppy is now left by itself it will be unlikely to chew the furniture because it will be worried that a cushion will fall on it from above.

Barking for attention

Once again let's look at the reason behind this behaviour. Look at it from the dog's point of view. Lots of puppies learn to bark at one another as an invitation to play a game of chase. When some puppies arrive in their new homes they bark at their owners as an invitation to play in the same way that they did with their brothers and sisters. If the owner then plays with the puppy, it will learn that by barking it can get the owners to speak to it and sometimes play. The problem is that this barking can easily become a nuisance and sometimes gets so bad that neighbours start to complain about the noise.

So you can see why it is important to teach your puppy that if it barks in order to try to get you to play, you will ignore it until it is quiet. The puppy should soon learn that this sort of barking does not get it the excitement that it wants.

Play-biting and nipping

Lots of owners end up with some of the more serious problems with their adult dogs simply because they allowed them to think that play-biting and nipping were acceptable whilst they were still puppies. Although your family and friends may not be too worried about your puppy playfully nipping at their fingers, you have to consider what will happen if the puppy still does this to visitors and friends when it is fully grown and has strong adult teeth. The rule you have to establish right at the start is that your puppy must not bite your fingers, or any other part of your body for that matter.

To stop this behaviour all you need to do is to dip your fingers into a small container of a special liquid known as a TASTE DETERRENT whenever it becomes excited and tries to play with your hands. The puppy will soon learn that you taste really nasty and will become less and less likely to 'mouth' at your hands in play.

More serious problems

And make sure your dog has plenty of rest....

It is fairly unusual for a dog to have any of the more serious problems described here, but it is important that you understand the danger signs to watch for in order to prevent an accident. If you have any of the following problems then you should take your puppy along to see your vet right away. Your vet will soon decide if your dog is feeling off colour, in which case he/she will treat it to cure the problem. If the vet decides your dog is perfectly healthy he/she might want you to go to see a person who specialises in these kinds of behaviour problems so that they can be put right as soon as possible.

Snapping

Most of the more serious problems of dogs snapping at people who approach them occur because they have been teased and tormented when they were puppies. The pup then quickly learns to snap at the offending hand in order to avoid being teased. To prevent this happening with your puppy it is important that you never allow anyone to tease it or to try and force themselves on it, particularly when the puppy is in an enclosed area. (See also 'Growling'.)

Growling

Growling is quite often a dog's way of warning people not to go near. If these warnings are ignored there is a very real danger that the dog may bite the person who is approaching. There are many reasons why a dog may growl. It may be feeling unwell and not want to be touched or moved. It may be frightened that you are going to tell it off, or it may be trying to be a bit bossy. If your puppy ever growls at you it is important that you tell your parents immediately. Never continue to approach your dog if it starts to growl at you. Never try to tell it off or, worse still, smack your dog if it growls at you.

If your dog gets a bit grumpy then these are the times and places that it will most likely growl at you, so try to avoid them until your parents have sorted these problems out: (a) when you stroke it when it is lying in its bed or any of its (or your) sleeping areas; (b) when you try to brush it, particularly behind the ears and anywhere near its tail, including the back legs; (c) when you try to get it down off a chair; (d) when the dog has stolen something that it is not supposed to have and you try to take it away from it; (e) when you try to tell the dog off; (f) when you try to make the dog lie down; (g) when you go near the dog when it is eating.

Owning a pet dog should be a pleasurable experience and you should make sure that you do not allow any problems of growling, snapping or biting to develop when it is a puppy. That would cause you to become frightened of the puppy when it grows into an adult dog.

7 Choosing an older dog

Some people decide to choose an older dog because they do not have the time that is necessary to bring up a young puppy. This means that they are generally looking for a dog that is over the chewing stage and is already house-trained. Although it is possible to go and get an older dog from a rescue kennels that is well behaved, it is not often that this happens. A recent study has been carried out by one of our leading animal charities. This showed that the reason that some people give their young dogs to these places is because they have had problems with their behaviour. Such behaviour has made them difficult to live with and control, but with the right help and advice, nearly all can become well-mannered companions.

If you decide to get a dog from a rescue centre you and your parents should be aware that some of these dogs have already had some bad experiences with people. These dogs have been rejected once already. It is not fair to take a dog just to see if it is going to be all right and then have to return it as unsuitable.

The problem is that when you go along to a rescue kennels you cannot usually tell, just by looking, what each dog is going to be like. You have to rely on the staff at the kennels to tell you if the dog has any problems. They only know what the original owner tells them and what

they have learnt from the way that it behaves in kennels. Sometimes what the owner tells the staff is not quite how the dog really behaves.

If you decide to try re-homing an older dog, the following notes should help you to decide which one is going to be the most suitable.

First of all sit down with the rest of your family and write down all the things that you think are important in deciding the type of dog that you want. This means details such as the type of coat and the size of the dog. Do you want a dog or a bitch? Do you want a lively dog or a quiet one? Also think about what age you would like your dog to be. Find the telephone numbers of your nearest animal charity or rescue kennels and give them a ring to see if they have a dog that meets your description. DO NOT go along to the kennels to have a look around and see the dogs. Otherwise you are certain to start feeling sorry for some of the dogs. Then you may end up taking one home that is totally unsuitable.

If the kennels have a dog that closely matches your description then the whole family should go along to see it. This will give you a good idea of what its behaviour may be like with all the people with whom it may be going to live. Some dogs are good with adults but dislike children (sometimes because a child has teased them). Some are all right with women but not friendly with men.

When you look at the dog in its kennel does it seem friendly with all of you? If so, ask the kennel staff to take the dog out of the kennel and brush it so you can see if it is easy or difficult to handle. If the dog growls or tries to bite when it is being brushed, do not choose that dog. Look for another one, because this indicates that this dog, even though it may look friendly at other times, may have quite serious problems.

If all goes well and you think that the dog is going to be suitable, ask the staff for as much information as possible about its background. You should not expect to be able to take the dog home right away. The kennels will want to do a home visit first to check that your home is going to be a suitable one for this particular dog. Remember that most rescue kennels have considerable experience in placing these dogs in the right homes, so be guided by their advice. It is given with the dog's and your interests at heart.

If your home is suitable then the staff will usually give you all the information that you need to help your dog settle in to your household. Make sure that you fully understand what is needed before you collect your dog.

When you take your dog home it is important to begin the first day the way you mean to go on. If you take your dog up to bed with you on its first night in order to help it to settle in, then the dog will expect to sleep in your bedroom every night. If the dog happens to be a bit bossy (dominant) then it may start to take advantage of you. So the kitchen may be the best choice for its sleeping area right from the first night.

Make up a list for all the family to follow of what the dog is and isn't allowed to do and make sure that you all follow it. It is unfair to set a rule for the dog to follow today and then change all the rules tomorrow.

You will have very little information on the dog's background and you will not know what rules it has learnt to understand. So you should behave in exactly the same manner as if it were a young puppy who has not learnt any rules at all. Don't think that the dog knows the meaning of simple commands such as 'Come' or 'Sit', because its previous owners may have used different words. It is up to you to teach the dog all over again so that it is not confused.

For the first two or three weeks do not make the mistake of thinking that you know the dog quite well. This means that you should not take unnecessary risks. You should never try to take food away from the dog when it is eating. You should not wrestle with the dog on the floor (you should NEVER do this). Neither should you stroke the dog when it is lying in its bed, nor cuddle it. Your parents should be the ones to make sure that your dog is completely safe and friendly before you take any risks. Remember that your dog may have been hurt when it was younger by a child who came up and cuddled it. So the dog may not want you to cuddle it.

After you have had the dog for two or three weeks, it should have settled in. You, and your family, should start to grow more confident about its behaviour. If you experience any problems then it is important that you get in touch with the kennel staff right away so that they can help you. Some animal welfare organisations such as the Blue Cross have behaviour experts that can help you to get the best out of your re-homed dog.

As long as you make sure that your parents are present whenever you are with your dog they will be able to make sure that the two of you learn to understand one another.

When you introduce your friends to your new dog, make sure that they do not approach it: you must read the next chapter and teach them how to let the dog approach them.

Also be sure not to give the dog too much fuss and attention for the first few days, otherwise the dog may find it very difficult to cope when it suddenly finds itself without your company when you go out to school. The dog may then become destructive when left on its own.

well, he's certainly settled in well.....

43

8 Making friends with other dogs

It is a sad fact that some children are bitten by pet dogs every year. This is simply because they failed to understand that dogs have a different language from our own. Also dogs have feelings such as fear and excitement that have to be understood. Most bites are completely avoidable if you obey a few simple rules. You should also help other children to apply these rules to your own pet dog.

People that have learnt how to communicate with dogs, such as vets, groomers and trainers, hardly ever get bitten, even though they may be dealing with dogs that are difficult to handle. The reason is that they have learnt to read the warning sounds and signals that the dog gives. These are known as BODY LANGUAGE and these signals tell them when a dog is safe to touch. If the dog is telling them that it is not safe to touch, then they will make sure that they do not handle that dog until it has been made safe to do so. They will make the dog safe to touch by putting a special bandage around its jaws, or a muzzle. They could even give the dog some medicine that will make it sleepy.

To reduce the likelihood of your ever being bitten by a dog you should learn how to approach and touch dogs. You should also learn what to do if a dog comes up to you and wants to say 'Hello'.

Dogs that are on the lead without their owners

You will often see dogs that are fastened up outside shops because many shops do not allow dogs to go inside. Although most of these dogs appear to be very friendly, it is wrong to go up and try to touch or stroke a dog when its owner is not with it. This is because when you approach, it may jump up to greet you and tangle its legs in the lead. It may then bite you because it thinks that you are hurting it. There are also some dogs that try to guard their leads and may be very protective when they are fastened up. It is also possible that the dog has a sore ear or a bad leg or other injury. It may then bite you when you touch a particularly sensitive area.

Dogs that are on the lead with their owners

The rule to follow here is always to ask the owner's permission first. The owner should know whether or not their dog is friendly towards children. They will only give permission if they know that it is safe to do so. If you are given permission to stroke the dog, then you will need to do it this way so that the dog realises that you are friendly. It will also give you the opportunity to see if the dog remains friendly.

Ask the owner what the dog's name is. Talk to the dog gently by speaking its name before you try to approach.

If the dog wags its tail and seems happy then you can put out one hand and let the dog come towards you to sniff it.

If the dog barks, growls or moves backwards then do not attempt to stroke it. Leave it alone, because it is telling you that it does not want to be touched, and you should respect its wishes.

If the dog comes forward and sniffs your hand, you can gently stroke it under the chin and throat. Watch its tail as you stroke its chin, and if it wags, you can continue.

If its tail stiffens and hardly moves or tucks right up under its tummy, then it is better not to stroke it any more. It is not enjoying being touched.

Make sure that you do not bend over the dog when you are stroking it. You should make sure that you do not bring your face close to the dog's face. You should avoid staring into its eyes because this will make it think that you are threatening.

All your stroking should be around its chest and sides: avoid touching it behind the ears or rear end. Only stroke its head if it accepts you touching its chest and sides.

Only stroke it for a short time. Make sure that you do not make the dog tired of being stroked.

Do not try to hold on to the dog's collar or restrain it in any way. If it pulls away from you at any stage then allow it to do so.

And finally NEVER put your arms around the dog and try to cuddle it.

Dogs that are off the lead

Never approach any dog that is off the lead. Any dog that is not with its owner is not under control, so leave these dogs well alone.

If you are approached by a dog that is off the lead, even if the owner is only a few yards away, then try to follow these rules. This will show the dog that you are not going to hurt it or play fighting or chasing games with it.

1. Stand perfectly still, facing the dog, but do not stare into its eyes.
2. Bring your hands slowly up and fold them across your chest, tucking your hands under your arms.
3. Do not try to run away, because the dog may think that you are playing games of chase or catch-me-if-you-can.
4. Pretend that you are a statue and the dog should quickly think that you are not worth bothering with and will soon lose interest and wander away.
5. When the dog has gone, you can slowly walk away.
6. If the dog was not with its owner, you should tell your parents as soon as you get home. It is against the law to allow a dog out by itself and it may get involved in an accident.
7. Never try to chase a dog away by shouting at it or waving your arms in the air.
8. If you are riding a bicycle and a dog starts to chase you then do not try to race it. Get off and position the bike between you and the dog, and it should soon go away.
9. If you see two dogs fighting, on no account should you attempt to separate them. Go and get help from a grown-up.
10. Never put your hand inside a car to touch a dog: it may have been left on guard.

Remember that nearly all dogs are friendly, but you also have to understand that some are not, and so you should never take any chances. Make a habit of using all the rules when you meet another dog. Help any of your friends to use the same rules when they meet your dog for the first few times. Then we can stop most cases of accidental bites.

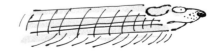

9 How much do you know about dogs?

These questions have been made up to test your understanding of dogs. They are split into ten sections: the first eight are about the information in each of the first eight chapters of this book, while the last two are general sections and you will need to borrow some books from your library to help you to answer some of them.

Dogs through the ages

1. Name two senses that your dog has which are better than your own.
2. Name the six GROUPS in which our breeds of dogs are placed.
3. What were two of the skills for which dogs were first kept so that they could practise them for their owners?
4. Name two breeds of herding dogs.
5. Which group of dogs are generally believed to have the best eyesight?
6. Into what group do retrievers and spaniels fit?

7. What was the terriers' original purpose?
8. Which dog is sometimes known as the Butterfly Dog?
9. The practice of breeding from carefully selected parents is known as…?
10. From which wild animals do our domestic dogs come?

So you want a puppy?

1. What is the difference between a crossbreed and a mongrel?
2. What is another name for a pure-bred dog?
3. If you have a male dog neutered what will this prevent?
4. Who in your family should choose the breed of dog that you get?
5. How long is a bitch usually in season?
6. How can you prevent a bitch from having litters of unwanted puppies?
7. For how many years can you expect a dog to live with you?
8. How can you find out more about the breeds in which you are interested?

9. What is a name that is used to describe a small, social group of dogs?
10. If you are going to allow your dog into the garden, what should you have done to stop it from escaping and causing an accident?

Choosing your puppy

1. How can you get a list of breeders?
2. Why are puppy farms usually not licensed?
3. Is it all right to buy a puppy from a pet shop?
4. How many visits should you make to the breeder before you buy a puppy?
5. Where is the best place to buy a crossbreed or mongrel puppy?
6. Who should go along to view the puppies?
7. If the breeder has difficulty in brushing the puppies' mother, what does that tell you about the pups?
8. What does a pedigree form show you?

9. Is it a good idea to take two puppies home as company for one another?
10. Who can register the puppy with the Kennel Club?

The early weeks

DOWN BOY!

1. What equipment should you have ready for the arrival of your puppy?
2. What should you do before you take it into your house?
3. At which times will your puppy be most likely to want to go to the toilet?
4. What should you put down at night when you leave your puppy in the kitchen?
5. Is it a good idea to allow your puppy to sleep in your bedroom?
6. Whom should you visit within two days of getting your puppy?
7. Is it all right to play with your puppy when there is not a grown-up present?
8. Name one thing that you and your parents need to do with your puppy every day to get it used to being handled.

9. Where can you find out about your nearest puppy playgroup?
10. What can you give your puppy to help it settle in during the first few nights that it is left by itself?

Training your puppy

1. Who will have the greatest responsibility for training your puppy?
2. What is physical praise?
3. What is verbal praise?
4. What is the first command that your puppy must learn to obey?
5. What does 'Down' mean when you are training your puppy?
6. For how long should your early training sessions last?
7. Is it all right to train only at weekends, when you are off school?
8. Can you train your puppy by itself without your parents being there?
9. If you play tugging games, where should the toy be when you are not playing with it?
10. Is wrestling or rough-and-tumble a good game to play with your puppy?

Bad behaviour

1. What sort of things should you NOT give your puppy to play with?
2. If your puppy barks at you to try to get you to play with it, what should you do?
3. Is it all right to allow your puppy to nip at your fingers when it is playing?
4. Where should you take your puppy for advice if it starts to growl or snap at you?
5. Give two reasons why your pup might growl at you.
6. If an action is rewarded what is likely to happen?
7. If you see your puppy chewing the carpet should you chase it around the room and shout at it?
8. If you and your friends do not mind your puppy play-biting your fingers, is it then all right to allow this to continue?
9. What is meant by 'environmental correction'?
10. If your dog growls at you occasionally, is it a good idea for you to brush it behind the ears and around its rear end?

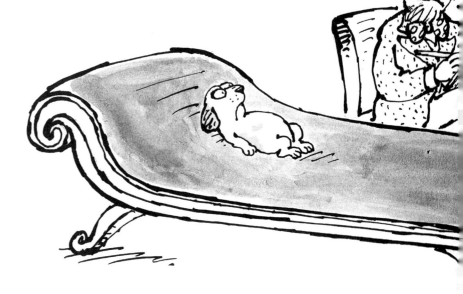

Choosing an older dog

Er.... Um.....

1. Are most of the dogs that end up in rescue kennels well-behaved?
2. Is it a good idea to go along to a rescue kennels to see if they have any dogs that you like?
3. What should you do if the dog that you choose tries to bite the kennel maid who tries to brush it?
4. Can you take a dog home from a rescue kennels straight away?
5. Would an older dog already know words such as 'Sit' or 'Come'?
6. Is it all right to lie on the floor and give a newly re-homed dog a cuddle to make it feel wanted?
7. How long will it take an older dog to settle into your home?
8. If you have problems with a re-homed dog's behaviour, whom should you contact?
9. Is it all right to allow this dog to sleep in the kitchen?
10. Do all dogs like children?

Zo, und ven did you start growling und snepping et your owner?....

Making friends with other dogs

You herd— I'll guard

1. What should you do if a dog chases you when you are riding a bicycle?
2. What should you do if you want to stroke a dog that is with its owner?
3. Is it all right to stroke a dog that is fastened on a lead whilst its owner is inside a shop?
4. If you get permission from its owner to stroke a dog, what should you do before you touch it?
5. Why should you not put your face close to a dog and stare into its eyes whilst you are stroking it?
6. If a dog comes rushing up to you and its owner is not in sight, what should you do with your hands?
7. Why should you not run away if a stray dog approaches you and barks?
8. What should you do if you see two dogs fighting?
9. Is it all right to stroke a dog that is inside a car by putting your hand through the window?
10. Do all dogs bite?

Health

Proper poorly!

1. How long does it take for a bitch to have a litter of puppies after she has been mated?
2. How often should your dog be wormed?
3. What are the four main diseases that your dog should be inoculated against?
4. How often will your dog need booster injections to keep it fully protected?
5. What is the normal temperature of a dog?
6. Should you brush a dog before or after bathing it?
7. If you find fleas on your dog how can you get rid of them?
8. At what age does a puppy open its eyes?
9. Which teeth would a dog use to catch and hold an animal or bird?
10. How many teeth does an adult dog have?

Responsible dog ownership

1. If you are out with your dog and it makes a mess on the footpath what should you do?
2. If your dog is very obedient, is it all right to allow it to walk along the pavement without a lead?
3. Where can you learn how to train your dog?
4. What should you do with your dog if you go abroad on holiday?

5. You already have one dog: is it a good idea to buy a second dog as company for it, because you do not have enough time to give to your dog yourself?
6. If you own a bitch that has a few problems, is it a good idea to breed a litter of puppies from her in order to settle her down a bit?
7. If your puppy makes a mess on the floor should you rub its nose in it?
8. If you do not have time to take your dog out for exercise is it all right to allow it out of the house by itself?
9. If you think that someone is ill-treating a dog (or any other animal) to whom should you report it?
10. Why is it dangerous to leave a dog in a car with the windows closed when it is sunny?

10 What your parents should know

One of the most important questions to ask yourself when deciding if a pet dog is going to be right for your family is WHY do we want a dog? The wrong reasons for wanting to own a dog are outlined below.

1. Never buy a dog just because a child has asked for one. The WHOLE family must want to own a dog. An adult must always accept the responsibility for a pet dog's welfare. It is unfair and unwise to allow a young child to take on this role.

2. Never buy a dog as a toy for a child to play with. Dogs have feelings, and a child has to learn to understand and respect these. Young puppies do not remain cute and cuddly for very long, and tens of thousands of young dogs are discarded every year, once the initial novelty has worn off, in the same way as an unwanted toy may be discarded when the child grows bored with it.

3. Never buy a dog on impulse. All puppies look cute and attractive in a pet shop window and the proprietor will play on the fact that we are born with a need to look after infants of any species. Many people take on a ten- to fifteen- year commitment in just one moment of madness. A decision taken in haste is likely to be regretted at your leisure.

4. Never buy a dog when a different type of pet would be more appropriate in your circumstances. You will need to invest more time and effort in keeping a pet dog than you will in keeping any other companion animal. Sometimes, by choosing a smaller, easier-to-manage pet, you can allow your child a far greater share of the responsibility for its welfare.

Once you have come to a decision to buy a puppy (or obtain an older dog), you will need to read through this book with your child in order to assist in answering the many questions that will surely arise.

The chapters have been written in a way that should arouse an interest in learning more about the relevant aspects of dog ownership. There is a wealth of information available for further study, and this is detailed under chapter headings below. When you read this book with your child it is important that you emphasise the most important points in each individual chapter.

Chapter 1

The ancestors of our domestic dogs lived a life that was to the mutual benefit of both parties. Like our dogs, we live in small social packs and so it is easy to see why two apparently different animals can live together as one. Although our many breeds of dog exhibit different shapes, sizes, colours and coat lengths, it has been demonstrated that over 80% of the behaviour traits of wolves are still to be found in the companion dogs of today.

Dogs are placed into groups depending on their original purpose. These groups will give you an indication of the likely characteristics of an individual breed.

Further reading

PETS ARE GOOD FOR PEOPLE Pedigree Petfoods information leaflet from the Talking Pets series.

PETS FOR CHILDREN   Pedigree Petfoods information leaflet from the Talking Pets series.

Chapter 2

When you have made a decision to get a puppy, you should encourage your children to discuss their likes and dislikes with you so that you can then start to look at breeds which may be suitable. It is important to note that the prime consideration when choosing a breed is whether or not that breed is appropriate for your lifestyle, means and experience. Some breeds are not recommended for first-time dog owners, whilst others have a predisposition for certain types of behaviour which you may find difficult to accept.

Further reading

WHAT DOG? MAGAZINE
Looks at breed traits and matches
breeds to environment.

PEDIGREE PETFOODS
SELECTADOG   Fill in a form
giving details of your house, family,
etc. and you will receive a list of
breeds suitable for your
environment.

A CODE OF CONDUCT FOR
PET OWNERS   Pedigree
Petfoods information leaflet from
the Talking Pets series.

Chapter 3

Always try to obtain a puppy from a
reputable breeder. If you then have
any difficulties the breeder will
either be in a position to help or will
certainly be able to put you in touch
with someone who can. The
foremost consideration when
selecting a puppy has to be its likely
temperament. The best indicator of
your puppy's temperament is an
observation of its mother in her
natural surroundings. It is for this
reason that the whole family must
go along to view the litter. You
should never buy a puppy as a
surprise for your children: if you do,
they may get more of a surprise
than you bargained for as the puppy
begins to grow.

Further reading

OUR DOGS or DOG WORLD
Weekly newspapers which carry
advertisements for puppies for sale
and breed societies.

Chapter 4

If you have chosen your puppy wisely, then the first six months of its life should be carefully planned to add to the experience that its mother, littermates and the breeder have already started. Early continual socialisation with people, other dogs and the environment is absolutely crucial if problems are to be avoided. Vaccines are being developed which enable puppies to be taken out and about as early as eight weeks of age, and you should take full advantage of this. More healthy dogs are destroyed each year because of behavioural problems due to lack of proper socialisation than are killed by the four main canine diseases.

Make sure that your children as well as your puppy understand the rules by which they are to live. This means that correct supervision is essential at all times, particularly during games.

Further reading

LOOKING AFTER YOUR PUPPY   Blue Cross information service booklet.

FEEDING YOUR DOG   Pedigree Petfoods information leaflet from the Talking Pets series.

TOILET TRAINING FOR DOGS Pedigree Petfoods information leaflet from the Talking Pets series.

Chapter 5

You will have the responsibility of training the puppy and also of teaching your children how the training is achieved. Training is not shouting commands and forcing your puppy to do things against his will. Training should be a pleasurable experience which is carried out using a system of rewards. The early training exercises that are so necessary for control are detailed on the wall-chart that you can send for, free from Pedigree Petfoods Education Centre. Once your puppy has mastered the basic exercises then you can allow your child to become involved in the training but this should always be supervised.

Further reading

TRAINING YOUR DOG Pedigree Petfoods information leaflet from the Talking Pets series.

Chapter 6

If you are having any behaviour problems with your dog, particularly any that involve aggression, then it is important that you seek professional help. Your vet is the first person to consult, because there are a number of problems that relate to a dog's physical well-being. If the problems are not due to physical causes then your vet may be able either to advise you himself or to refer you to a recognised behaviour counsellor in your area. You should never anticipate that your young dog will grow out of problems as it matures: problems of aggression invariably get worse unless treated. It is also important that you do not breed from a dog that is exhibiting any form of problem behaviour, in the belief that it will have a calming effect: it won't!

Further reading

THE GOOD BEHAVIOUR GUIDE   A booklet written by a behaviourist in an easy-to-read style. Available from Dog Help, Upper Street, Defford, Worcestershire WR8 9AB.

Chapter 7

A survey carried out by one of the leading animal welfare groups found that over 33% of all owners that give their dogs up for re-homing cite behaviour problems as the reason why they want to part with their pets. The reason that people sometimes choose an older dog rather than a puppy is because they want a dog that is past the chewing and house-training stage. These are the very reasons why some dogs end up in rescue, because they are not house-trained or because they are destructive when left. In the vast majority of cases it is this type of behaviour that can very easily be corrected provided that (a) the new owner is informed of the problem and (b) appropriate advice is given by the re-homing organisation, so as to give the new owner the best possible chance to re-educate the dog, thereby avoiding the possibility of problems developing within the new home.

Further reading

YOUR RE-HOMED DOG   Blue Cross information leaflet.

Chapter 8

The idea of this chapter is to educate children on the right and wrong way to approach dogs in order to minimise any possible danger of a child misinterpreting a dog's 'body language'. Many children are bitten each year through ignorance of how and when to touch a dog and most of these incidents are avoidable. You must remember that ALL dogs can bite, although the vast majority won't, despite the almost incredible amounts of intimidation that some get from children. Teach your child to respect all dogs, and teach your dog to respect all children.

Further reading

MAKE FRIENDS WITH DOGS Co-op education leaflet. Available from Mrs J. Thompson, Penrose Cottage, Withiel, nr Bodmin, Cornwall PL30 5NP.

Chapter 9

The questions are designed to test your child's knowledge of each chapter in turn. The answers are all contained within the chapters, and re-reading a chapter should be encouraged in cases of difficulty. The sections on 'Health' and 'Responsible Dog Ownership' contain questions that cannot be answered by reading this book, but your child should be encouraged to find the answers by reading the many leaflets and booklets listed in this chapter, most of which can be obtained free of charge by writing to the addresses listed in the Appendix.

Books for further reading

Bower, J.S.M. & Youings, D. *The Health of Your Dog* (Crowood Press) 1989

British Veterinary Association *BVA Guide to Dog Care* (Dorling Kindersley) 1989

Edney, A.T.B.; Ed. *Dog & Cat Nutrition* (Pergamon Press) 1988

Edney, A.T.B. & Mugford, R.A. *The Practical Guide to Dog and Puppy Care* (Salamander) 1987

Evans, J.M. & White, K. *The Book of the Bitch* (Henston) 1988

Evans, J.M. & White, K. *The Doglopaedia* (Henston) 1985

Fisher, John *Think Dog* (H.F. & G. Witherby) 1990

Fogle, Bruce *The Dog's Mind* (Pelham) 1990

Hartmann-Kent, Sylvia *Your Dog and Your Baby* (Doghouse Publications) 1990

Holmes, John *The Family Dog* (Popular Dogs) Tenth edition 1991

Neville, Peter *Do Dogs Need Shrinks?* (Sidgwick & Jackson) 1991

O'Farrell, Dr Valerie *Problem Dog: Behaviour and Misbehaviour* (Methuen) 1990

Palmer, J. *A Dog Owner's Guide to Training Your Dog* (Salamander) 1987

Patmore, Katie *So Your Children Want a Dog?* (Popular Dogs) 1991

Rogerson, John *Training Your Dog* (Popular Dogs) 1992

Rogerson, John *Understanding Your Dog* (Popular Dogs) 1991

Rogerson, John *Your Dog: Its Development, Behaviour and Training* (Popular Dogs) 1988

Ruiz, S. *A Dog Owner's Guide to Grooming Your Dog* (Salamander) 1987

Turner, Trevor, Ed. *Veterinary Notes for Dog Owners* (Popular Dogs) 1990

Appendix

Useful addresses

Blue Cross, Shilton Road, Burford,
Oxfordshire 0X18 4PF.

The Kennel Club, 1 Clarges Street,
Piccadilly, London WlY 8AB.

Association of Pet Behaviour Counsellors,
257 Royal College Street, London NWl.

Pedigree Petfoods Education Centre, PO Box 77,
Freepost, Burton-on-Trent DE11 7BR.

Pet Plan Insurance, Freepost,
319-327 Chiswick High Road, London W4 4BR.

Puppy Sleep Tapes, 10 Guest Lane, Silkstone,
Barnsley, South Yorkshire S75 4LF.